Drops Shopify: Ultimate Guide to Succeeding in the Lucrative E-commerce Market

From Beginner to Advanced - Strategies, Tactics, and Secrets to Start & Skyrocket Your Shopify Store Revenue $M

Brad V. Guy

Copyright © 2023 by Brad V. Guy

All rights reserved. No part of this publication may be reproduced, distributed, or transmitted in any form or by any means, including photocopying, recording, or other electronic or mechanical methods, without the prior written permission of the publisher, except in the case of brief quotations embodied in critical reviews and certain other noncommercial uses permitted by copyright law.

Dedication

This guide is dedicated to all those who are earning daily from dropshipping and the tender inquisitive hearts that desire to be among these league.

Table of Contents

1. Introduction   4
   - Why Dropshipping on Shopify in 2024 is a Lucrative Opportunity
2. Understanding Dropshipping   8
   - Understanding what dropshipping is and how how it works
   - Advantages and Disadvantages of Dropshipping
3. Setting Up Your Shopify Store   13
   - Choosing the Right Niche
   - Selecting a Profitable Product Inventory
   - Designing an Eye-Catching Storefront
   - Optimizing the User Experience
4. Sourcing Products for Your Store   20
   - Finding Reliable and Trustworthy Suppliers
   - Evaluating Product Quality and Pricing
   - Retaining Control over Inventory and Logistics
5. Managing Orders and Fulfillment   27
   - Setting Up Automated Order Processes
   - Tracking and Managing Inventory
   - Implementing Effective Fulfillment Strategies
6. Marketing and Promoting Your Store   35
   - Crafting appealing product descriptions and visuals
   - Driving Traffic through Effective Social Media Marketing
   - Implementing SEO Strategies for Organic Growth
   - Leveraging Influencer Marketing for Maximum Exposure
7. Customer Service and Retention   50
   - Providing Excellent Customer Support

- Building credibility and fostering customer loyalty for yourself
   - Implementing Effective Refund and Return Policies
8. Scaling Your Business   58
   - Analyzing Data to Optimize Performance
   - Identifying Opportunities for Expansion
   - Automation and Outsourcing for Growth
9. Key Challenges and How to Overcome Them   68
   - Dealing with Seasonality and Market Trends
   - Managing Inventory and Stockouts
   - Handling Customer Complaints and Disputes
10. Financial Management and Profit Maximization   78
   - Pricing Strategies for Competitive Advantage
   - Cost Optimization and Margin Improvement
   - Tracking Expenses and Revenue
   - Strategies for Increasing Profitability
11. Future Trends and Strategies   89
   - Adapting to Evolving E-Commerce Trends
   - Exploring New Opportunities and Platforms
12. Conclusion   96
   - Recap of Key Learnings
   - Tips for Success in Dropshipping on Shopify in 2024

INTRODUCTION

Why Dropshipping on Shopify in 2024 is a Lucrative Opportunity

Welcome to "Dropshipping Shopify 2024," your comprehensive guide to creating a successful dropshipping business on the Shopify platform. In this book, we will cover everything you need to know to start your own profitable online store, even if you're a complete beginner.

If you find yourself belonging to one or more of these categories, then this guide is perfect for you.

- A complete newbie in the world of dropshipping
- Someone who wants to gain more knowledge and understanding in dropshipping
- An entrepreneur looking to scale up their dropshipping business
- Someone seeking to enhance their dropshipping skills and strategies
- And many more!

I will take you step by step and show you how to make a fortune from this business. You can check the table of contents to have an overview of what you're going to learn.

One thing that I need from you is **IMPLEMENTATION**! As you go through this guide, don't just read but implement or make plans on how to implement what you'll be learning. With that in mind, let's get started...

Nowadays, e-commerce has become an integral part of our lives, with more people than ever before opting to shop online. This shift in consumer behavior presents a tremendous opportunity for aspiring entrepreneurs like you to tap into the booming e-commerce industry. And one of the most popular and low-risk ways to get started is through dropshipping.

What exactly is dropshipping? It's a business model that allows you to sell products without having to worry about inventory management, fulfillment, or shipping. Instead of purchasing and storing inventory upfront, you work with suppliers who will ship the products directly to your customers on your behalf. This means you can focus on marketing, customer service, and growing your business, while leaving the logistics to others.

So, why is dropshipping on Shopify such an exciting opportunity, especially in 2024? The answer lies in the platform's immense popularity and advanced features that enable entrepreneurs to create a professional online store quickly and easily. Here are a few reasons why dropshipping on Shopify in 2024 is a lucrative opportunity:

1. Shopify's User-Friendly Interface: Shopify is renowned for its user-friendly interface, making it accessible to beginners and experts alike. You don't need to be an experienced web developer or designer to create a visually appealing and functional online store. With its drag-and-drop website builder and customizable themes, you can have your store up and running in no time.

2. Integration with Third-Party Apps: Shopify offers a wide range of apps and plugins that can enhance the functionality of your store. From marketing tools and analytics to inventory management and customer service, you can find the right apps to streamline your business operations and drive growth.

3. Extensive Payment Options: Shopify integrates with various payment gateways, providing customers with a seamless and secure checkout experience. By offering multiple payment options, you can cater to customers' preferences, ultimately boosting conversion rates and increasing sales.

4. Shipping and Fulfillment Solutions: Shopify's built-in shipping features and integration with leading fulfillment services help streamline the logistics of your dropshipping business. You can easily track orders, manage inventory, and automate the fulfillment process, freeing up your time to focus on scaling your business.

5. Robust Analytics and Reporting: Shopify provides detailed analytics and reporting tools that give you valuable insights into your store's performance. By analyzing this data, you can make informed decisions to optimize your marketing strategies, product selection, and pricing, ultimately maximizing your revenue.

6. Active Community and Support: Shopify has a vibrant community of entrepreneurs and experts who are eager to help and share their knowledge. Whether you have questions about setting up your store or need advice on marketing, you'll find a wealth of information and support within the Shopify community.

Dropshipping on Shopify in 2024 presents an incredibly lucrative opportunity to build a successful e-commerce business. With Shopify's user-friendly interface, integration with third-party apps, extensive payment options, shipping and fulfillment solutions, robust analytics, and supportive community, you have all the tools you need to turn your entrepreneurial dreams into reality.

In the following chapters, I will guide you step-by-step through the process of setting up your Shopify store, sourcing products, managing orders, marketing your store, providing excellent customer service, scaling your business, and maximizing your profit potential. So buckle up and get ready to embark on an exciting journey into the world of dropshipping on Shopify in 2024!

All I need from you is to implement all you're going to learn here and you will soon share your testimony at the review session.

Chapter 2: Understanding Dropshipping

Understanding what dropshipping is and how how it works

Imagine a world where you can run a successful e-commerce business without worrying about inventory, packaging, or shipping. It seems like a dream come true for you, right? Well, that dream is called dropshipping.

Dropshipping is an e-commerce business model that allows entrepreneurs to run a store without the hassle of stocking products or dealing with complex logistics. In a traditional retail model, the store owner would need to purchase inventory upfront, store it, and ship it to customers when they make a purchase. With dropshipping, you don't have to worry about any of this.

Here's how it works:
1. You set up an online store: Using platforms like Shopify, you can easily create a professional-looking online store. This will act as your digital storefront.

2. Find reliable suppliers: Once you have your store set up, it's time to find suppliers who are willing to dropship their products. These suppliers will handle the inventory and shipping on your behalf.

3. List products on your store: You can now choose products from your suppliers' catalogs and list them on your Shopify store. When a customer makes a purchase, you will receive the payment.

4. Place orders with suppliers: Once you have received the payment from your customer, you will place an order with your supplier. They will then package and ship the product directly to your customer's doorstep.

5. Profit: The difference between the price you charge your customer and the price you pay your supplier is your profit. It's that simple!

Advantages and Disadvantages of Dropshipping

Now that you understand the basics of dropshipping, let's discuss some of the advantages and disadvantages associated with this business model. Like any other business, dropshipping has its pros and cons, and being aware of them will help you make informed decisions.

Advantages:
1. Low startup costs: Dropshipping offers the benefit of requiring only a small initial investment, making it an attractive option due to its low startup costs. You don't need to purchase inventory or rent a warehouse, making it a cost-effective option for aspiring entrepreneurs.

2. Easy to get started: Setting up a dropshipping store is relatively easy, especially with user-friendly platforms like Shopify. You don't need any technical expertise or a big team to get started.

3. Flexibility and scalability: Dropshipping allows you to run your business from anywhere in the world with an internet connection. You are not bound to a physical location, and you can easily scale your business by adding more products or targeting new markets.

4. Wide product selection: With dropshipping, you have access to a wide variety of products from various suppliers. This gives you the freedom to cater to different customer preferences and tap into trending niches.

Disadvantages:
This shouldn't discourage you, but like everyother business, they're disadvantages. The rule is that if you perceive that the advantages is more than the disadvantages, then you head right in. And I can tell you that it is so here in dropshipping and if you follow the steps I'm going to show you in this guide, you will surely join those who have made a fortune from dropshipping.

So here are few disadvantages
1. Lower profit margins: Since you don't produce the products yourself, the profit margins in dropshipping tend to be lower compared to traditional retail. You'll need to find ways to optimize your operations and drive higher sales volume to compensate for this.

2. Dependency on suppliers: Your business is reliant on your suppliers to fulfill orders accurately and on time. If your supplier runs out of stock or fails to meet customer expectations, it reflects poorly on your brand.

3. Increased competition: Dropshipping has gained popularity over the years, resulting in increased competition. It can be challenging to stand out in a crowded market, so you'll need to develop a strong marketing strategy to attract customers.

4. Limited control over customer experience: Since you're not handling the shipping and packaging, you have limited control over the customer experience. Any issues with delivery or product quality will need to be resolved through your supplier.

While dropshipping offers many advantages, it's important to understand the potential challenges before diving in. With the right approach and a willingness to learn and adapt, dropshipping can be a rewarding business venture.

But with this guide, you have nothing to fear. You will learn how to conquer and earn high revenue like never before (if you already started) and how to start out and earn high (if you're just a newbie).

In the next chapter, we will dive into the process of setting up your Shopify store and discuss the essential steps you need to take to ensure its success. So, grab a cup of coffee, and get ready to embark on an exciting e-commerce journey!

Chapter 3: Setting Up Your Shopify Store

Congratulations on taking the first step towards building your own successful online store! In this chapter, we will focus on the essential elements of setting up a Shopify store. We'll explore how to choose the right niche and select a profitable product inventory. So, let's get started!

Choosing the Right Niche

Finding the right niche is crucial for the success of your Shopify store. A niche is a specific market segment within a broader industry. You want to find a niche that has a sufficient demand but isn't overly saturated with competition. Here's how you can achieve the right niche:

1. Identify your interests and passions: Start by understanding your own interests and hobbies. What are you passionate about? This will help you stay motivated and engaged with your store.

2. Research market trends: Use tools like Google Trends, social media platforms, and online forums to explore trending topics and consumer interests. Look for niches that are growing in popularity or have a loyal customer base.

3. Analyze competition: Take a look at your potential competitors in the niche you're interested in. Are they successful? Can you find ways to differentiate yourself and offer a unique selling proposition?

4. Consider profit potential: Research the potential profit margin for the products in your chosen niche. Are people willing to spend money on these items? Make sure there's room for profit after accounting for product costs, marketing expenses, and other overheads.

Selecting a Profitable Product Inventory

Once you've chosen a niche, the next step is to curate a product inventory that will attract customers and generate revenue. Here's how you can do achieve this:

1. Conduct thorough market research: Dive deep into your chosen niche to understand the kinds of products that are in demand. Look for gaps in the market or products with limited competition.

2. Source products from reliable suppliers: Consider using dropshipping to fulfill your orders. This allows you to partner with suppliers who handle inventory management and shipping, minimizing your upfront costs and logistics. Conduct thorough research to find reliable suppliers that provide top-notch products

3. Verify product quality: Before listing any product in your store, request samples from potential suppliers to ensure they meet your standards. Test their shipping times, packaging quality, and overall customer experience.

4. Assess profit margins: Calculate the potential profit margins for each product you plan to sell. Consider the cost of the product, shipping fees, and any additional expenses like packaging or branding. Aim for products that offer a reasonable profit margin while remaining competitive with similar offerings in the market.

5. Offer a varied product range: Consider offering a range of products within your niche to cater to different customer preferences. This can help boost your chances of making sales and increase customer satisfaction.

Remember, product selection is an ongoing process. Continuously monitor your sales data, customer feedback, and industry trends to refine your product inventory over time.

By carefully choosing the right niche and selecting a profitable product inventory, you'll lay a solid foundation for your Shopify store. Next let's dive into designing an eye-catching storefront and optimizing the user experience. So, keep reading, and get ready to make your Shopify store stand out from the crowd with this expertise!

Designing an Eye-Catching Storefront

Here, let's dive into the essential steps required to design an eye-catching storefront and optimize the user experience of your Shopify store. Remember, a visually appealing and user-friendly storefront can greatly impact your potential customers' first impression and encourage them to stay and explore your products. So let's get started!

1. Choose a Clean and Modern Theme:

When selecting a theme for your Shopify store, opt for a clean and modern design. Look for themes that align with your brand identity and provide a seamless browsing experience for your customers. Shopify offers a range of free and paid themes, so explore different options and choose the one that complements your products.

2. Create a Compelling Logo:

A logo acts as your brand's visual representation. It helps establish brand recognition and builds trust with your customers. Use a logo maker tool or hire a designer to create a professional logo that represents your brand's personality. Place your logo prominently on your storefront to increase brand visibility.

3. Use High-Quality Product Images:

Compelling high-quality product images are crucial for attracting & enticing potential customers. Invest in product photography or use stock images that accurately showcase your products. Ensure that the images are clear, well-lit, and showcase your products from different angles. Avoid using blurry or pixelated images as they can negatively impact your store's credibility.

4. Organize Your Products:

Structure your product categories in a logical manner, making it easy for visitors to navigate your store. Use clear and concise category and product names that accurately describe what you're selling. Consider using subcategories to further organize your products and make it easier for customers to find what they're looking for.

Optimizing the User Experience

1. Streamline the Checkout Process:

Make the checkout process simpler by reducing the number of necessary steps. Avoid asking for excessive information and only request what's necessary for order fulfillment. Consider implementing guest checkout options and offer multiple secure payment gateways to accommodate your customers' preferences.

2. Implement a Search Function:

Including a search bar in your Shopify store allows customers to quickly find specific products. Ensure that the search bar is easily visible and consistently present on all pages of your store. Additionally, optimize your store's search function by enabling features such as autocomplete and product suggestions.

3. Enhance Website Speed:
Page loading time can greatly impact user experience. Optimize your store's speed by compressing images, minimizing code, and choosing a reliable web host. Slow-loading pages can frustrate potential customers and increase the likelihood of them leaving your store without making a purchase.

4. Ensure Mobile Responsiveness:
With the increasing use of smartphones, it is crucial to optimize your store for mobile devices. Choose a responsive theme that can automatically adapt to layout and design depending on the user's device. Test your store on various mobile devices to ensure a seamless and user-friendly experience for your mobile customers.

5. Include Customer Reviews and Ratings:
Building trust and credibility by displaying customer reviews and ratings can greatly benefit your business. Use apps or plugins to incorporate review sections on product pages and encourage customers to leave feedback after making a purchase. Positive reviews can influence potential customers' purchasing decisions and increase your store's conversion rate.

By implementing these strategies, you can create an eye-catching storefront and optimize the user experience in your Shopify store. Remember to regularly monitor and analyze your store's performance, make necessary adjustments, and stay updated with the latest trends in e-commerce design. A visually appealing and user-friendly store will enhance your brand's reputation and increase the chances of converting visitors into loyal customers.

Stay tuned for the next chapter, where we will explore source quality products that will attract traffic to your Shopify store!

Chapter 4: Sourcing Products for Your Store

Congratulations on setting up your Shopify store (that is if you are following this course step by step and have set up your own store)! Now that your store is up and running, it's time to start thinking about sourcing products to sell. One of the key aspects of running a successful dropshipping business is retaining control over inventory and logistics. Finding reliable and trustworthy suppliers is essential for a successful dropshipping business. Additionally, evaluating product quality and pricing will help ensure customer satisfaction and profitability. This chapter will guide you through the process of finding reliable suppliers and managing your inventory and logistics effectively. Let's dive in and discover the steps to sourcing products effectively.

Finding Reliable and Trustworthy Suppliers

When sourcing products for your Shopify store, it's crucial to work with reliable and trustworthy suppliers. Here are a few proven methods to find the right suppliers:

1. Use Supplier Directories: Online supplier directories like Alibaba, Oberlo, and SaleHoo provide a wide range of suppliers for various products. These directories allow you to filter suppliers based on location, price, and their expertise. Carefully review supplier profiles, ratings, and customer reviews to ensure their credibility.

2. Attend Trade Shows: Trade shows are great platforms to meet potential suppliers in-person, establish connections, and evaluate the quality of products firsthand. Research industry-specific trade shows and network with suppliers who meet your criteria.

3. Reach Out to Manufacturers: If you have a particular product in mind, consider contacting the manufacturers directly. Manufacturers often have a list of authorized distributors or can refer you to reliable suppliers. A straightforward Google search or industry-specific forums can help you identify manufacturers to reach out to.

4. Join Online Communities: Engage with online communities and forums related to your niche. Gain insights from fellow entrepreneurs and ask for supplier recommendations. Participating in these communities can lead you to trustworthy suppliers who have already been vetted by other dropshippers.

Evaluating Product Quality and Pricing

Once you've identified potential suppliers, it's crucial to assess both the product quality and pricing to make informed decisions. This is how you can examine these aspects effectively:

1. Request Samples: Before partnering with a supplier, order product samples to assess their quality. This step allows you to evaluate the material, construction, packaging, and overall product experience. Remember, delivering quality products to your customers is vital for the success of your business.

2. Compare Prices: Don't settle for the first supplier you come across. Reach out to multiple suppliers and compare their pricing structures. Note that the cheapest prices are not always the best option. Consider factors like quality, shipping times, customer support, and any additional fees they may charge.

3. Check Supplier Ratings and Reviews: Online directories and platforms often provide supplier ratings and customer reviews. Take the time to read through these reviews to understand the experiences of other dropshippers who have worked with the suppliers you are considering. Look for suppliers with positive feedback and a high level of reliability.

4. Communicate with the Supplier: Contact potential suppliers with any questions you may have regarding their products, policies, and order processing times. Prompt and informative responses indicate that the supplier is attentive and reliable. Communication is key to building a healthy supplier partnership.

By combining these methods, you'll be well on your way to finding reliable suppliers who offer quality products at competitive prices. Remember, taking the time to research and evaluate suppliers will contribute to the long-term success of your dropshipping business.

Next, let's discuss how to retain control over inventory and logistics, ensuring smooth operations and customer satisfaction.

Retaining Control over Inventory and Logistics

Retaining control over inventory means ensuring that the products you sell are in stock and readily available to your customers. In the dropshipping model, you don't hold physical inventory, so it's essential to partner with suppliers who are reliable and can fulfill your orders promptly. To find trustworthy suppliers, you can start by exploring reputable supplier directories like Oberlo, SaleHoo, or AliExpress. These platforms provide access to a wide range of suppliers who are experienced in dropshipping.

When evaluating potential suppliers, there are a few factors to consider. First and foremost, assess their product quality. It's vital to maintain a high level of customer satisfaction, so it's essential to work with suppliers who offer quality products. You can order samples from potential suppliers to test their products firsthand. This allows you to assess the product's quality, packaging, and how long it takes for the sample to arrive.

Additionally, consider the supplier's pricing structure. Ensure that the pricing is competitive and allows you to maintain a reasonable profit margin. Compare prices from different suppliers and make sure to factor in any additional costs such as shipping fees and taxes.

Another crucial aspect of retaining control over inventory and logistics is having clear communication with your suppliers. Establish a good working relationship with them and communicate your expectations regarding order fulfillment, shipping times, and any special requirements. Regularly check in with your suppliers to assess their performance and address any concerns promptly.

By maintaining control over inventory, you'll be able to offer accurate and up-to-date product availability information to your customers. Your Shopify store can be integrated with various inventory management apps that sync your store with your suppliers' inventory. With the help of these apps, you'll be able to automatically update the stock levels on your store based on the information provided by your suppliers.

Managing logistics efficiently is crucial for delivering a great customer experience. When it comes to shipping, it's essential to choose reliable shipping methods offered by your suppliers. Look for shipping options that provide tracking information, reasonable delivery times, and competitive rates. This information can be displayed on your store to set clear expectations for your customers.

To further streamline your logistics, consider offering multiple shipping options to your customers. This allows them to select the delivery method that is most convenient for them. Additionally, provide clear and accurate shipping information to your customers, such as estimated delivery times and tracking numbers. This helps build trust and transparency, which are essential for a successful dropshipping business.

Another key aspect of managing logistics effectively is dealing with returns and refunds. Make sure you have a clear and customer-friendly return policy in place. Establish guidelines for returns, exchanges, and refunds, and communicate this information clearly on your store. Promptly address any customer concerns or issues related to product quality or delivery problems.

To summarize, retaining control over inventory and logistics is essential for running a successful dropshipping business. Partner with reliable suppliers who offer quality products at competitive prices. Maintain clear communication with your suppliers, regularly assess their performance, and keep an eye on your inventory levels. Streamline your logistics by offering multiple shipping options, providing accurate shipping information to your customers, and having a customer-friendly return policy in place.

By implementing these strategies, you'll be able to ensure a smooth and efficient operation of your dropshipping business, providing an excellent experience for your customers and increasing your chances of success.

Chapter 5: Managing Orders and Fulfillment

In this chapter, we will delve into the crucial aspects of managing orders and fulfillment in your dropshipping Shopify store. These are key components in ensuring smooth operations and customer satisfaction. We will cover three important areas: Automated order process, tracking and managing inventory, and implementing effective fulfillment strategies.

Setting Up Automated Order Processes

Congratulations on starting your Shopify store! Now that you have your products listed and your store set up, it's time to focus on managing orders and ensuring smooth fulfillment for your customers. In this chapter, we will explore the importance of setting up automated order processes and how you can implement them effectively.

Why Set Up Automated Order Processes?

As your store grows and more orders start coming in, managing them manually can quickly become overwhelming. This is where integrating automation comes to the rescue. By automating your order processes, you can save time, reduce errors, and provide a better customer experience.

Automated order processes enable you to streamline order fulfillment, reduce administrative tasks, and improve efficiency. They allow you to handle a large volume of orders seamlessly and deliver them to your customers promptly. This can help increase customer satisfaction and boost your store's reputation.

Here are some key steps to set up and automate your order processes effectively:

1. Order Notifications: Enable Shopify's email notifications to keep you and your customers informed about order status updates. Customers will receive order confirmation emails, while you can receive notifications for new orders, canceled orders, and shipment updates. This keeps everyone in the loop and reduces the need for manual follow-ups.

2. Order Fulfillment Apps: Shopify offers various apps that integrate with your store and automate the fulfillment process. These apps can connect to your suppliers, track inventory, generate shipping labels, and update customers with tracking information. Research and choose an app that suits your business needs and integrates seamlessly with your store.

3. Inventory Management: Proper inventory management is crucial in dropshipping. You need to ensure that your suppliers have sufficient stock to fulfill orders. Again, there are apps available that can sync your inventory with your suppliers' inventory and provide real-time updates. This helps prevent overselling and enables you to fulfill orders accurately.

4. Tracking Orders: Keeping your customers informed about the status of their orders is vital. With automated order processes, tracking information is updated automatically through the integration with your chosen order fulfillment app. This allows customers to track their orders independently, reducing the need for constant inquiries and improving their shopping experience.

5. Handling Returns and Refunds: Establish clear policies for returns and refunds to provide a hassle-free experience for your customers. While automation may not cover all aspects of returns and refunds, having well-defined procedures in place will help you handle them more efficiently and maintain customer satisfaction.

Proven Strategies for Effective Automation

Now that you understand the importance of setting up automated order processes, let's explore some proven strategies to make the most of this automation:

1. Test and Optimize: Once you have set up your order automation systems, test them thoroughly to ensure they work as expected. Place test orders and go through the entire fulfillment process to identify any issues or potential improvements. Continuously optimize your automation workflows to make them even more efficient.

2. Integration with Suppliers: Establish effective communication channels with your suppliers and ensure seamless integration between their inventory management systems and your store. This will help you avoid stockouts, mishaps, and delays. Regularly check stock levels and update your inventory information accordingly.

3. Customer Communication: While automation can handle order notifications and tracking updates, it's still essential to maintain clear and prompt communication with your customers. Include relevant contact information and provide additional channels for support, such as live chat or email. Personalized customer service goes a long way in building trust and loyalty.

4. Stay Up-to-Date: E-commerce and dropshipping are constantly evolving. Keep up to date with the latest trends, regulations, and best practices to stay ahead. Regularly review your order automation processes and explore new tools and technologies to enhance your store's efficiency and customer experience.

Remember, effective automation is a continuous process. As your business grows and evolves, you may need to adapt and optimize your order processes accordingly.

Next, let's delve into tracking and managing inventory, another crucial aspect of successful dropshipping. Stay tuned to learn how you can keep track of your stock levels, prevent overselling, and ensure timely fulfillment for your customers.

Tracking and Managing Inventory

One of the essential elements of successful dropshipping is efficient inventory management. You need to keep track of your products, their availability, and ensure accurate updates on your website. Here's how you can effectively manage inventory for your Shopify store:

1. Centralize Inventory Management: To avoid confusion and potential errors, it's recommended to centralize your inventory management. This means syncing your inventory across all sales channels, including your online store, marketplaces, and any other platforms where you sell your products. Shopify offers various apps and integrations that can help you achieve this, such as Oberlo, Inventory Source, or Dropified.

2. Regularly Update Inventory: It's crucial to keep your inventory levels up-to-date to prevent overselling or disappointing customers with out-of-stock products. Make it a habit to update your inventory regularly, especially after each sale or when you restock. Many Shopify apps, like the ones mentioned earlier, can help automate this process by syncing your inventory in real-time.

3. Set Low Stock Alerts: Avoid unexpected stockouts by setting up low stock alerts. Many inventory management tools and Shopify apps allow you to define a minimum inventory threshold for each product. When stock levels reach or fall below this threshold, you'll receive a notification to initiate restocking.

4. Utilize Inventory Reports: Shopify provides insightful inventory reports, giving you a comprehensive overview of your product performance. These reports can help you identify top-selling items, slow-moving products, and trends to make informed decisions regarding inventory management, pricing, and marketing.

Implementing Effective Fulfillment Strategies

Efficient fulfillment processes are vital to provide an excellent customer experience and maintain a positive reputation for your dropshipping store. Below are some strategies to consider for effective fulfillment:

1. Assess Shipping Options: Research and evaluate different shipping carriers to find the most reliable and cost-effective options for your business. Compare shipping rates, delivery times, and customer reviews to determine which carriers align with your needs.

2. Offer Tracking Information: Transparency is key when it comes to order fulfillment. Provide your customers with tracking information so they can track their shipments' progress. This helps build trust and ensures customers can anticipate delivery dates.

3. Automate Order Processing: Streamline your order processing by automating repetitive tasks. Shopify offers features that allow you to automate order fulfillment, such as order status updates, sending tracking information to customers, and generating invoices.

4. Communicate with Customers: Keep your customers informed throughout their journey, from purchase to delivery. Send timely order confirmation emails, update them on the fulfillment progress, and provide tracking details. Clear communication helps manage expectations and reduces customer inquiries.

5. Monitor and Resolve Order Issues: Occasionally, issues may occur, such as lost packages, damaged items, or delayed deliveries. Stay vigilant by monitoring order progress and promptly resolving any issues that arise. Use customer support channels to address concerns professionally and effectively.

6. Establish Relationships with Suppliers: Building strong relationships with your suppliers is crucial for ensuring timely order processing and resolving any supply-related issues promptly. Good communication and reliability go a long way in maintaining a healthy supplier partnership.

By effectively tracking and managing inventory while implementing efficient fulfillment strategies, you can optimize your dropshipping operations for success. Remember, consistently evaluating and adapting these processes will contribute to a seamless customer experience, leading to positive reviews, repeat business, and ultimately, the growth of your Shopify store.

Continue in the next chapter for tips on how to market and promote your store for massive sales in your dropshipping venture.

Chapter 6: Marketing and Promoting Your Store

Congratulations on setting up your professional Shopify store! (I keep congratulating you because you're on a your journey to daily income and dropshipping mastery. Dropshipping is worth this price if you master all I'm teaching you now).
Now that your store is ready to go, it's time to focus on driving traffic and generating sales.

Crafting appealing product descriptions and visuals

When it comes to running a successful dropshipping store on Shopify, one of the key factors that can make or break your sales is your product descriptions and imagery. Since you don't physically own the products you sell, it's essential to present them in a way that captures your customers' attention and compels them to make a purchase. In this section, we will dive into the art of creating compelling product descriptions and imagery that will help drive conversions and boost your revenue.

Creating Engaging Product Descriptions
1. Know your target audience: Before crafting your product descriptions, it's important to understand your target audience and their needs. Research their demographics, interests, and pain points to tailor your

messaging accordingly. Use language that resonates with them and addresses their specific pain points or desires.

2. Highlight key features and benefits: Focus on the unique selling points of your products and convey them clearly in your descriptions. Highlight the benefits your customers will gain by using the product and how it solves their problems or improves their lives. Be specific and include important details like materials, colors, sizes, and any special features.

Instead of simply stating "This t-shirt is comfortable," enhance your description by highlighting specific features. For instance, you can say "Crafted from premium organic cotton, this t-shirt provides unbeatable comfort, making it ideal for all-day wear."

3. Tell a compelling story: Create an emotional connection with your customers by incorporating storytelling elements into your product descriptions. Describe how the product has positively impacted the lives of others or share a personal experience related to the product. By tapping into your customers' emotions, you can increase their desire to own the product.

4. Use persuasive and descriptive language: Use powerful and persuasive words to captivate your readers. Words like "exclusive," "limited edition," "must-have," or "best-selling" can evoke a sense of urgency and exclusivity. Include sensory and evocative language to help customers envision themselves using the product. Paint a vivid picture through words.

5. Include social proof: People trust the opinions of others, especially when making online purchases. Incorporate customer testimonials, reviews, ratings, or endorsements to add credibility to your product descriptions. Social proof can help alleviate any doubts or concerns potential customers may have and increase their confidence in your store.

Creating Eye-Catching Product Imagery
1. Invest in high-quality visuals: High-resolution product images are crucial to catching your customers' attention and conveying the quality of your products. If possible, hire a professional photographer to create stunning visuals that showcase your products from multiple angles. Alternatively, you can also use stock photos or contact your suppliers for high-quality product images.

2. Use consistent branding: Create a visually cohesive and consistent brand image throughout your store. Use the same color scheme, fonts, and design elements for your product images to strengthen your brand identity. Consistency in branding helps build trust and recognition among your customers.

3. Show the product in action: Instead of solely relying on static product images, consider incorporating lifestyle photos or videos that demonstrate the product being used. This allows customers to visualize how the product fits into their lives and increases their desire to own it.

4. Optimize image files for faster loading: Slow-loading images can frustrate customers and lead to abandoned carts. Compress your image files without compromising quality to ensure fast loading speeds on your website. Use image optimization tools or plugins available on Shopify to streamline this process.

5. Provide zoom-in functionality: Enable your customers to explore the product details by offering a zoom-in feature on your product images. This gives them a closer look at the product, enhancing their confidence in making the purchase.

Remember, compelling product descriptions and visually appealing imagery are crucial to engaging potential customers and driving conversions. Invest time and effort into creating content that aligns with your target audience's needs and desires. Consistency in branding and high-quality visuals will help you build trust and credibility, leading to a successful dropshipping business on Shopify.

Next, let's explore how to drive traffic to your store through effective social media marketing.

Driving Traffic through Effective Social Media Marketing

One powerful strategy to achieve traffic generation is through effective social media marketing. In this section, we will dive into the world of social media marketing and provide you with practical tips and strategies to make the most out of your online presence.

Understanding Social Media Marketing

Social media platforms like Facebook, Instagram, Twitter, and Pinterest have billions of active users, which makes them an ideal place to promote your store and products. The idea behind social media marketing is to leverage these platforms to build brand awareness, engage with your target audience, and ultimately drive traffic to your Shopify store.

Choosing the Right Social Media Platforms

To begin, you need to identify which social media platforms are most suited to your target audience and products. Conduct market research to understand where your potential customers spend their time and tailor your social media strategy accordingly. For example, if you sell trendy fashion accessories, platforms like Instagram and Pinterest may be your go-to choices due to their highly visual nature.

Creating Engaging Content

Once you've determined the appropriate platforms, it's time to create engaging and shareable content. High-quality visuals, including product photos and lifestyle images, are essential for catching your audience's attention. Showcasing your products in action, highlighting their features, and demonstrating their value can help drive interest and encourage sales.

To create compelling content, consider investing in professional photography or use image editing tools to enhance your images. Be sure to maintain a consistent visual theme and branding across all your social media channels to establish a sense of professionalism and build recognition.

Building a Social Media Community

Building a loyal social media community around your brand is crucial for its long-term success. Encourage your followers to engage with your content by asking questions, conducting polls, and responding to comments promptly. This fosters a sense of inclusion and encourages people to share your content and spread the word about your products.

Running Contests and Giveaways

Running contests and giveaways on social media can be an effective way to increase your following and generate buzz around your brand. Craft enticing offers that encourage users to participate, such as "tag a friend to enter" or "share this post for a chance to win." This not only increases engagement but also exposes and opens up your brand to new potential customers.

Paid Advertising on Social Media

While organic reach is valuable, investing in paid social media advertising can significantly boost your store's visibility. Social media platforms offer various ad formats, including sponsored posts, carousel ads, and video ads, which allow you to target specific demographics, interests, and behaviors.

When running paid ads, it's essential to monitor their performance closely. Analyze metrics such as click-through rates, conversion rates, and the return on ad spend (ROAS) to optimize your campaigns and maximize your budget.

Collaborating with Influencers
Influencer marketing has become a popular and highly effective way to promote products and reach a wider audience. Collaborating with influencers who align with your brand can help build credibility, generate trust, and drive more traffic to your Shopify store.

Begin by identifying influencers within your niche who have an engaged following and reach out to them with genuine, personalized messages. Offer them your products in exchange for a review, shoutout, or sponsored post. When working with influencers, ensure that their values align with your brand's image and that their audience matches your target market.

Measuring and Analyzing Social Media Performance
To ensure your social media efforts are paying off, it's crucial to measure and analyze your performance. Utilize the analytics tools provided by each platform to monitor key metrics, such as follower growth, engagement rates, and click-through rates. These insights will help you understand what content resonates

with your audience and which strategies are driving the most traffic and sales.

Social media marketing is a powerful tool in your arsenal for driving traffic and increasing sales for your Shopify store. By creating engaging content, building a community, running contests, investing in paid advertising, and collaborating with influencers, you can effectively promote your products and reach a wider audience. Remember to continuously analyze your social media performance, adapt your strategies accordingly, and stay consistent with your brand messaging. With dedication and continuous improvement, social media marketing can be a game-changer for your dropshipping business.

Implementing SEO Strategies for Organic Growth

Now that your store is ready for business, it's time to learn about implementing SEO strategies to drive organic growth. SEO (Search Engine Optimization) can significantly impact your store's visibility on search engines like Google, Bing, and Yahoo, leading to increased traffic, higher conversion rates, and ultimately, more sales.

1. Conduct Keyword Research:
Keyword research is the foundation of SEO. It involves identifying the words and phrases your potential customers are searching for online. Start by

brainstorming a list of relevant keywords and then use keyword research tools like Google Keyword Planner, Ubersuggest, or SEMrush to expand your list and discover new targeted keywords. Look for keywords with high search volume, low competition, and relevance to your products. For example, if you sell eco-friendly kitchenware, focus on keywords like "sustainable kitchenware" or "eco-friendly utensils."

2. Optimize Your Product Pages:
After pinpointing & identifying your target keywords, it is necessary to optimize your product pages. Start by incorporating your keywords strategically into your product titles, descriptions, and image alt tags. However, avoid keyword stuffing, as this can lower your rankings. Craft unique, compelling, and informative product descriptions that not only appeal to search engines but also engage your potential customers. Include relevant details, benefits, and specifications, using your keywords naturally throughout the content.

3. Create Informative Blog Content:
Blogs are a fantastic way to enhance your store's SEO and provide valuable information to your audience. Write engaging and informative blog posts related to your niche, products, and industry. Incorporate relevant keywords into your blog post titles, headers, and body content. Ensure your blog posts are well-structured and easy to read, with bullet points, subheadings, and appropriate internal and external links. This will encourage others to link to your content, improving your store's authority and visibility in search engine rankings.

4. Build High-Quality Backlinks:
Backlinks are links from other websites that direct users to your store. They're one of the most critical factors in SEO, as search engines view them as a vote of confidence for your content. Concentrate on establishing strong backlinks from reputable websites in your specific field & industry. You can achieve this by reaching out to influencers, industry bloggers, or relevant publications, requesting them to link to your store. Additionally, guest blogging on authoritative websites can help you earn backlinks and increase your store's visibility.

5. Optimize Your Store's Loading Speed:
The speed at which a page loads is a critical aspect that impacts both user experience and SEO. A slow-loading website can decrease your rankings and increase bounce rates. Optimize your store's loading speed by compressing images, minifying code, enabling browser caching, and choosing a reliable hosting provider. Regularly monitor your website's loading speed using tools like Google PageSpeed Insights or GTmetrix, and make necessary optimizations to improve user experience and search engine rankings.

6. Leverage Local SEO:
If you have a physical store or target customers in a specific geographical area, optimizing your website for local SEO is crucial. Include your business address, phone number, and opening hours on your website and

create a Google My Business listing. This will help your store appear in local search results, increasing your visibility to potential customers in your area.

7. Monitor and Analyze Your Performance:
SEO is an ongoing process, and it's essential to monitor and analyze your store's performance regularly. Utilize tools like Google Analytics and Shopify's built-in analytics to track your website's traffic, conversion rates, and keyword rankings. Identify top-performing keywords and pages and optimize them further. Stay updated with changes in search engine algorithms and adjust your SEO strategies accordingly.

Remember, SEO takes time and patience. Results may not be immediate, but with consistent implementation of these strategies, you can experience steady organic growth and reach a broader audience over time. By investing in SEO, you'll position your store for long-term success and stand out from the competition.

Next, let's discuss another powerful marketing technique: leveraging influencer marketing for maximum exposure. Hope you're implementing?

Leveraging Influencer Marketing for Maximum Exposure

In today's digital age, influencer marketing has become a powerful tool for promoting products and gaining brand exposure. By collaborating with influencers who have a large following on social media, you can tap into their engaged audiences and generate interest in your Shopify store. In this chapter, we'll explore how you can leverage influencer marketing to maximize exposure for your dropshipping business.

1. Identify Relevant Influencers: The first step in leveraging influencer marketing is to identify influencers who align with your niche and target audience. Start by researching popular influencers in your industry or niche through platforms like Instagram, TikTok, YouTube, and blogs. Look for influencers with a significant number of engaged followers and whose content resonates with your brand.

2. Evaluate Influencer Credibility and Engagement: Once you've identified potential influencers, it's essential to evaluate their credibility and engagement. Take a closer look at their follower count, likes, comments, and shares on their posts. A high number of followers does not necessarily indicate a high engagement rate, so focus on influencers who have an active and engaged audience.

3. Establish a Connection: Building a genuine relationship with influencers is crucial for successful collaborations. Follow them on social media platforms, engage with their content by liking and commenting, and share their posts. This initial interaction helps to establish rapport and grab their attention before reaching out for potential partnerships.

4. Craft a Compelling Collaboration Proposal: When you're ready to reach out to an influencer, make sure your collaboration proposal is persuasive and compelling. Start by showing appreciation for their content and explaining how your brand aligns with their audience's interests. Highlight the benefits they can expect from collaborating with your dropshipping store, such as affiliate commissions or free merchandise. Personalize your approach and make it clear how their participation will be mutually beneficial.

5. Collaborate on Authentic Content Creation: To maximize the impact of your influencer partnership, encourage the influencer to create authentic and engaging content that showcases your products. Provide clear guidelines on the type of content you'd like them to create, whether it's a product review, unboxing video, or lifestyle photos featuring your products. Remember that transparency is key, and influencers should disclose any sponsored content for the sake of trust and authenticity.

6. Track and Measure Results: Throughout the collaboration, it's crucial to track and measure the results to evaluate the success of your influencer marketing campaign. Set specific goals and key performance indicators (KPIs) to monitor the impact of the campaign. Track metrics such as website traffic, conversions, social media engagement, and the number of sales generated. Analyzing this information will enable you to evaluate the success & effectiveness of your influencer collaborations and make informed choices for future partnerships.

7. Explore Micro-Influencers and Nano-Influencers: In addition to partnering with macro-influencers who have a massive following, consider collaborating with micro-influencers and nano-influencers. These influencers might have a smaller follower count but tend to have highly engaged and loyal audiences. Their recommendations can carry significant weight and be more effective in driving targeted traffic to your Shopify store.

8. Maintain Long-Term Relationships: Building long-term relationships with influencers can have a substantial impact on your brand's visibility and credibility. Once you've successfully collaborated with an influencer, continue to nurture the relationship by staying in touch and supporting their work. Periodically reach out for further collaborations, as they can provide ongoing exposure and cultivate a community of loyal customers around your brand.

Influencer marketing can be a highly effective strategy for increasing exposure and driving traffic to your Shopify store. By partnering with trusted individuals who have a dedicated following, you can tap into their influence and generate interest in your dropshipping products. Remember to focus on authenticity, build genuine relationships, and regularly track your campaign's performance. With time and effort, your influencer marketing efforts can result in significant revenue growth and a thriving online business.

Proof of successful influencer collaborations can be found in many case studies and success stories. For instance, the beauty brand Glossier gained widespread popularity by leveraging influencer marketing, resulting in a loyal and dedicated customer base. The electronics company DJI utilized influencers to promote their drones, leading to increased brand recognition and a surge in sales. These examples demonstrate the power and potential of influencer marketing if implemented strategically.

By following the steps outlined in this chapter and adapting them to your specific dropshipping niche, you can position your Shopify store for maximum exposure and success in the competitive e-commerce landscape. Keep in mind that influencer marketing requires careful planning, thorough research, and ongoing evaluation of results to ensure optimal outcomes.

Chapter 7: Customer Service and Retention

Providing Excellent Customer Support

When running a dropshipping business on Shopify, one of the essential factors for success is providing excellent customer support. Building a strong relationship with your customers not only leads to increased sales but also encourages them to become loyal repeat buyers. In this section, we will discuss some key strategies to offer exceptional customer support.

1. Prompt and Friendly Communication:
Timely and friendly communication is vital in creating a positive customer experience. It is important to promptly address customer inquiries, aim to respond within 24 hours ideally. Make sure to use a friendly and professional tone in your communication, addressing their concerns in a helpful manner.

2. Personalized Approach:
Treat each customer as an individual, not just another transaction. Address them by their name and customize your responses based on their specific queries. Personalization helps customers feel valued and appreciated, leading to higher satisfaction levels.

3. Clear and Transparent Policies:
Ensure that your terms, conditions, and policies are clearly displayed on your website. This includes shipping, return, and refund policies. By providing transparency, you build trust and manage customer expectations effectively.

4. Easy-to-Find Contact Information:
Make it easy & convinient for customers to reach out to you - contact you. Display your contact information prominently on your website, including an email address and phone number. Consider adding a live chat feature to provide real-time assistance, as this can significantly improve customer satisfaction.

5. Knowledgeable Staff:
Make sure to equip your customer support team with comprehensive training and extensive knowledge about your products. This will enable them to deliver accurate and valuable information to customers. Invest time in training your staff to handle customer queries efficiently.

Building credibility and fostering customer loyalty for yourself

Building trust and loyalty with your customers is crucial in maintaining a successful dropshipping business. Trustworthy brands not only attract new customers but also retain existing ones. Here are some strategies to build trust and loyalty with your customers:

1. Deliver on Your Promises:
Ensure that you deliver products promptly and as described on your website. Keep customers informed about shipment tracking details and any delays. If you consistently meet or exceed customer expectations, it will build trust and credibility - so aim at that.

2. High-Quality Products:
Only work with reputable suppliers who provide high-quality products. Conduct thorough research to avoid selling low-quality or counterfeit items. Offering genuine and durable products helps solidify your reputation and gain customer trust.

3. Product Reviews and Testimonials:
Encourage your satisfied customers to leave positive reviews and testimonials on your website or popular review platforms. These reviews act as social proof and can influence potential customers to trust your brand.

4. Loyalty Programs and Discounts:
Reward your repeat customers with loyalty programs or exclusive discounts. Offering incentives for their continued support not only encourages loyalty but also increases customer retention.

5. Social Media Engagement:
Engage with your customers on social media platforms. Respond to comments and direct messages promptly and maintain an active presence by sharing relevant content. Building a community around your brand helps foster loyalty and trust.

Providing excellent customer support and building trust and loyalty with your customers are crucial elements of a successful dropshipping business. By implementing the strategies outlined in this section, you can create a positive customer experience, resulting in increased sales, customer retention, and a flourishing Shopify store.

Remember, building a strong relationship with your customers takes time and dedication. Consistently delivering exceptional customer support and following through on your promises will help you establish a reputable brand that customers can trust.

Implementing Effective Refund and Return Policies

Welcome to this third and final section of Chapter 7! In this section, Let's delve into the importance of implementing effective refund and return policies in your dropshipping business. These policies are crucial for building trust with your customers and creating a positive shopping experience. So, let's get started!

1. Why are refund and return policies important?

When it comes to online shopping, customers want to feel confident about their purchases. Having clear and fair refund and return policies in place will help alleviate any concerns or doubts they may have. These policies are necessary to ensure customer satisfaction and build a foundation of trust between you and your customers.

By offering hassle-free refund and return options, you demonstrate your commitment to customer service, which encourages repeat purchases and word-of-mouth recommendations. Remember, happy customers are more likely to become loyal customers and advocates for your business.

2. Crafting an effective refund policy

a. Be transparent and clear: Create a refund policy that is easily accessible on your website. Clearly state the conditions under which refunds are granted, such as damaged or defective items, wrong sizes or colors, or failed deliveries. Ensure your policy is easy to understand, avoiding complex legal jargon.

b. Set a reasonable time frame: Define a timeframe within which customers can request refunds. Typically, this is 30 days from the date of purchase. Clearly communicate this window to avoid confusion. However, be open to flexibility if special circumstances arise.

c. Simplify the process: Provide a straightforward process for customers to request refunds. This could include a dedicated email address, a customer service form on your website, or even a live chat feature. Respond to refund requests promptly and professionally.

d. Review and analyze: Regularly review your refund policy to identify any recurring trends or issues. This analysis will help you identify areas for improvement in your product quality, packaging, or shipping methods.

3. Implementing an efficient return policy

a. Clearly define return conditions: Clearly outline the reasons for which customers can initiate returns, such as defective products or wrong items shipped. Ensure your return policy is easily accessible on your website and avoid any hidden or complicated terms.

b. Provide return labels: Make the return process as simple as possible for the customer by providing prepaid return labels. This eliminates any additional costs or inconvenience for the buyer, increasing the likelihood of them choosing to return.

c. Streamline the return process: Create a smooth and efficient return process that minimizes the efforts required from your customers. Provide detailed instructions on how to return items, including the address and any additional information required.

d. Promptly process returns: Once the returned merchandise is received, ensure you promptly process the refund or ship a replacement product. This helps in maintaining customer satisfaction and trust which should be one of your major goals.

4. Learn from returns and refunds

a. Track reasons for returns: Keep a record of the reasons for returns to identify any patterns or recurring issues. This will enable you to address these problems proactively and improve your overall product offering.

b. Use feedback to improve: Reach out to customers who initiate returns to understand their concerns and gather feedback. This information is invaluable for identifying areas where you can make improvements to prevent future returns.

c. Leverage return data for product selection: Analyze return data to identify any consistently problematic products. This information can help you adjust your product selection strategy for better customer satisfaction.

Remember, implementing effective refund and return policies is not just about adhering to legal requirements, but also about creating a positive customer experience. By providing transparent and hassle-free processes, you build trust and loyalty among your customers, ultimately leading to a successful and profitable dropshipping business.

I hope this section has provided you with the knowledge and guidance you need to implement effective refund and return policies in your dropshipping business. Remember, customer satisfaction should always be your top priority, and by prioritizing their needs, you are setting yourself up for long-term success.

Chapter 8: Scaling Your Business

Analyzing Data to Optimize Performance

Congratulations! By this point, you've successfully set up your Shopify store and have started generating some revenue through the dropshipping e-commerce business model. Now it's time to take things to the next level and scale your business for even greater success. Before diving into strategies for expansion, it's crucial to analyze your data and optimize your performance to ensure a solid foundation for growth. In this section, we'll explore the importance of data analysis and how it can help you make informed decisions to improve your business.

Analyzing your data provides valuable insights into customer behavior, sales patterns, and the overall performance of your Shopify store. With this information, you can identify areas for improvement, make data-driven decisions, and ultimately optimize your business operations. Let's dive into the key steps you can take to effectively analyze your data and maximize your business's potential.

Step 1: Define Key Performance Indicators (KPIs)
Before diving into data analysis, it's crucial to establish the key performance indicators (KPIs) that align with

your business goals. KPIs are specific metrics that allow you to measure and track the performance of various aspects of your business. Some common KPIs for an e-commerce store include conversion rate, average order value, customer acquisition cost, and customer lifetime value. By defining these KPIs, you'll have a clear understanding of what to analyze and measure to gauge your store's performance.

Step 2: Collect and Organize Your Data
To effectively analyze your data, it's essential to have accurate and organized information at your fingertips. Thankfully, Shopify provides built-in analytics tools that make this process relatively simple. Utilize these tools to gather data on sales, customer behavior, website traffic, and more. Additionally, you can integrate various third-party analytics tools to get a comprehensive view of your business performance. Ensure that you regularly collect and organize your data for meaningful analysis.

Step 3: Identify Trends and Patterns
With your data collected and organized, it's time to dive in and identify trends and patterns within the information. Analyze your sales data to identify the top-performing products, peak selling times, and popular customer demographics. Understanding these trends will help you optimize product offerings, create targeted marketing campaigns, and tailor your store's user experience to better serve your customers. Take note of any patterns that emerge and use them as a foundation for strategic decision-making.

Step 4: Perform A/B Testing

A/B testing is a valuable tool for optimizing various aspects of your Shopify store. It involves comparing two versions of a webpage, advertisement, or marketing campaign to see which performs better. By conducting A/B tests on elements such as product descriptions, images, pricing, and calls to action, you can gather data on what resonates most with your audience. Implement changes based on the results of your tests, and continuously refine and optimize your store for maximum impact.

Step 5: Utilize Customer Feedback

In addition to analyzing quantitative data, it's essential to gather qualitative data from your customers. Encourage feedback through post-purchase surveys or by providing a means for customers to leave reviews on your website. Customer feedback can provide valuable insights into pain points, satisfaction levels, and areas for improvement. Use this feedback to make data-backed decisions and continuously enhance your customers' experience.

Step 6: Set Goals and Monitor Progress

To stay on track with your growth plans, it's crucial to set measurable goals and monitor your progress over time. Determine specific targets related to sales, website traffic, conversion rates, or any other relevant KPIs. Regularly analyze your data to assess your performance against these goals and make adjustments as needed. This iterative approach to goal setting and monitoring will keep you focused on your objectives and help you make data-driven decisions to optimize your business.

Remember, data analysis is an ongoing process. Continuously reviewing and analyzing your data will provide you with invaluable insights to fuel your business's growth. By understanding customer behavior, optimizing key metrics, and using the information you collect to inform your decision-making, you'll be well on your way to scaling your dropshipping Shopify business and generating even greater revenue.

Next, let's delve into identifying opportunities for expansion, as well as automation and outsourcing strategies to facilitate your business's growth. Stay tuned for more insights and tips to supercharge your Shopify store!

Identifying Opportunities for Expansion

It's time to take your business to the next level and explore opportunities for expansion. Scaling your business is crucial for increasing your profits and reaching a larger customer base. In this section, we'll delve into the various strategies you can employ to identify opportunities for expansion.

1. Analyzing Customer Behavior and Trends:
One of the most effective ways to identify growth opportunities is by studying customer behavior and market trends. Analyzing data from your Shopify store

can provide valuable insights into your customers' preferences, buying habits, and popular products. Utilize tools like Google Analytics or Shopify's built-in analytics to gain a deep understanding of your customers' demographics, the channels they use to reach your store, and the products they purchase most frequently. With this knowledge, you can identify potential gaps in the market, target specific customer segments, and optimize your product offerings.

2. Conducting Market Research:
Take the time to research your competitors and analyze the broader marketplace. Explore other successful stores within your niche to identify products or strategies that are generating high demand. Keep an eye on emerging trends and new technologies that could open up new opportunities. Stay connected with industry-related blogs, forums, and social media groups to gain insights from fellow entrepreneurs and customers. By staying proactive and aware of industry developments, you can position your store to capitalize on emerging market trends.

3. Expanding Product Offerings:
Consider expanding & diversifying your product range to reach a wider audience of customers and cater for a broader customer base. Analyze your current product range and identify complementary products that align with your brand and customer preferences. By diversifying your product catalog, you can increase the likelihood of upselling and cross-selling, which can significantly boost your revenue. However, be cautious

not to deviate too far from your niche and dilute your brand identity. Maintain a careful balance between expanding your product range and staying true to your target audience.

4. International Expansion:
If your current store operates primarily within a specific market, consider expanding internationally. International markets offer immense potential for growth, as there are billions of potential customers outside your home country. Conduct market research to identify countries or regions where your products could be in high demand. Evaluate factors such as cultural differences, shipping costs, and local regulations before expanding to new markets. Shopify provides various apps and plugins that can simplify the process of reaching a global audience.

5. Collaborations and Partnerships:
Explore partnership opportunities with other businesses within your niche or complementary industries. Collaborations can open up new avenues for growth by leveraging the existing customer base of your partners. Look for brands or influencers with similar values and target audiences to create mutually beneficial partnerships. This could include guest blogging, joint promotions, or cross-branding initiatives. By leveraging the reach of other established businesses, you can attract new customers and increase your brand exposure.

Remember, scaling your business requires careful planning and execution. While the strategies outlined above can help you identify opportunities for expansion, it's essential to test and measure the success of each initiative. Continuously monitor your key performance indicators (KPIs) and make data-driven decisions to optimize your growth strategies.

With a thoughtful approach to scaling your business, you can reach new heights of success in the lucrative world of dropshipping. Keep exploring, adapting, and learning from your experiences to stay ahead of the competition and secure a profitable future for your Shopify store.

Next, let's discuss the important aspects of automation and outsourcing to facilitate your business's growth. Stay studying and implementing!

Automation and Outsourcing for Growth

Like I said earlier, now that you have successfully set up your dropshipping Shopify store and have started generating revenue, it's also time to think about scaling your business. As your business expands, it can become overwhelming to manage every aspect on your own. This is where automation and outsourcing can play a crucial role in your growth strategy.

Automation and Outsourcing for Growth

1. Automating repetitive tasks: One of the key benefits of automation is that it frees up your time to focus on more important aspects of your business. Identify tasks that are repetitive and time-consuming, such as order fulfillment, inventory management, and customer support. You can use various tools and apps available on the Shopify App Store to automate these tasks. For example, Shopify's order fulfillment app can automatically send tracking information to your customers, saving you valuable time.

2. Streamline your inventory management: As your business grows, keeping track of inventory can be a challenge. Automated inventory management systems can help you stay on top of your stock levels, ensuring that you never run out of popular products. These systems can also provide insights into sales trends, allowing you to make data-driven decisions when it comes to restocking or introducing new products. Consider using inventory management apps like Stock Sync or TradeGecko to streamline this process.

3. Outsource customer support: Providing excellent customer support is crucial for the success of your business. However, as your customer base grows, it may become difficult to handle all the inquiries and support requests on your own. Outsourcing customer support to virtual assistants or specialized customer service companies can ensure that your customers receive prompt assistance, even during busy periods. These professionals can handle tasks such as responding to emails, live chat support, and order inquiries, allowing you to focus on other aspects of your business.

4. Partnering with fulfillment centers: As your order volumes increase, it may become more efficient to partner with a fulfillment center. These centers can store your inventory, pick and pack orders, and handle shipping on your behalf. This can save you time and money, as they often have negotiated rates with shipping carriers. Shopify has integrated partnerships with various fulfillment centers, so you can easily connect and sync your orders with them. Examples include ShipBob, Rakuten Super Logistics, and Fulfillment by Amazon (FBA).

5. Hiring virtual assistants: Another option for outsourcing tasks is to hire virtual assistants (VAs). Virtual assistants can help with various aspects of your business such as product research, content creation, social media management, and customer support. Websites like Upwork and Fiverr provide platforms to connect with VAs with different skill sets. Be clear about the tasks you need assistance with and ensure good communication to establish a successful working relationship.

6. Test and refine: As you automate and outsource various aspects of your business, it's important to monitor and analyze the results. Keep track of key metrics such as customer satisfaction, response times, order processing time, and overall business performance. Analyze this data regularly and make adjustments as needed to optimize your workflows and ensure the quality of outsourced tasks. This continuous improvement mindset will help you refine and enhance your business operations over time.

By embracing automation and outsourcing, you can significantly streamline your business processes and focus on strategic growth. Remember, it's important to start small and gradually implement these strategies as your business grows. Don't forget to test and monitor the results consistently, and be open to refining your approach. With these tools in your arsenal, you'll be well-equipped to scale your dropshipping Shopify store and generate even greater revenue in the future.

Chapter 9: Key Challenges and How to Overcome Them

Dealing with Seasonality and Market Trends

One of the key challenges you'll face as a dropshipper is dealing with seasonality and market trends. The e-commerce industry is highly influenced by various factors, including seasonal demand, changing consumer preferences, and evolving market trends. To succeed as a dropshipper in the long run, it's crucial to understand how to navigate through these challenges and adapt your business accordingly.

1. Understanding Seasonality:
As a dropshipper, it's important to recognize that different products have varying degrees of seasonality. Certain items, such as swimwear or Christmas decorations, experience peak demand during specific times of the year. Understanding the seasonal patterns of your products will help you anticipate demand and plan your inventory accordingly.

To effectively deal with seasonality:
- **Analyze historical sales data**: Review sales data from previous years to identify any recurring seasonal trends. This information will help you plan your inventory levels and marketing efforts more effectively.

- **Forecast demand**: Use tools like Google Trends or social media listening to gauge consumer interest and predict demand for specific products throughout the year. By staying ahead of trends, you can adjust your product offerings and marketing strategies accordingly.

2. Adapting to Market Trends:
The e-commerce landscape is constantly evolving, and market trends can significantly impact consumer preferences and buying behaviors. To stay relevant and competitive, it's essential to keep an eye on emerging trends and adapt your dropshipping business accordingly.

Here's how you can adapt to market trends:
- **Stay informed**: Regularly keep up with industry news and trends through resources like social media, industry publications, and online forums. Look for emerging product categories, changing consumer behaviors, or shifts in popular sales channels.
- **Conduct market research**: Utilize market research tools and platforms to identify potential gaps or untapped opportunities in the market. By understanding consumer needs and preferences, you can adjust your product selection or target new customer segments to meet demand.
- **Test new products**: Continually test new product ideas and assess their potential success before fully committing to them. This can involve conducting small-scale trials, running targeted ads, or leveraging influencers to gauge consumer interest and gather feedback.

3. Diversify your product offerings:
One effective way to combat seasonality and market trends is by diversifying your product offerings. Instead of relying solely on one product or niche, consider expanding your range to cater to different customer needs throughout the year.

Here's how you can diversify your product offerings:
- Identify complementary products: Look for products that naturally complement your existing offerings. For example, if you're dropshipping fitness apparel, consider adding related accessories or workout equipment to your inventory.
- Introduce evergreen products: Include a selection of evergreen products that have consistent demand regardless of season or market trends. These can serve as reliable sources of revenue during slower periods.
- Stay flexible: Monitor your sales data and make data-driven decisions to optimize your product mix. Keep experimenting with new products and niches to find the right balance for your business.

Remember, adapting to seasonality and market trends is a continuous process. Stay agile, keep monitoring consumer preferences, and be open to adjusting your strategies as needed. By staying ahead of these challenges, you'll position your dropshipping business for long-term success.

Managing Inventory and Stockouts

In the world of dropshipping, managing inventory and avoiding stockouts is crucial to the success of your business. Inventory management entails keeping track of your products, ensuring their availability, and minimizing the risk of running out of stock. In this section, we will explore some effective strategies to manage your inventory and mitigate the impact of stockouts.

1. Accurate Product Monitoring:
To effectively manage your inventory, it's essential to have a clear understanding of your product performance. Start by tracking key metrics such as sales volume, conversion rates, and customer demand for each SKU (stock keeping unit). This data will serve as a foundation for making informed inventory decisions.

With the help of analytics tools or built-in reports in your Shopify store, you can gain insights into which products are selling well and which ones need attention. By regularly monitoring product performance, you can identify trends, plan for future demand, and adjust your inventory levels accordingly.

2. Real-Time Inventory Sync:
To avoid stockouts and overselling, it is essential to keep your inventory synced across all sales channels. This means that whenever a product is sold on your online store, the quantity is automatically updated in your inventory management system. By employing tools like

Shopify's inventory management features or third-party applications, you can ensure accurate inventory tracking in real time.

Real-time inventory synchronization not only prevents stockouts but also helps you manage customer expectations. Customers appreciate transparency, and knowing that a product is out of stock before they place an order leads to a positive shopping experience. Remember, happy customers are more likely to come back and refer others to your store.

3. Cultivate Supplier Relationships:
Building strong relationships with your suppliers is vital for efficient inventory management. Regular communication and clear expectations can help you maintain inventory levels that meet customer demand while avoiding excessive stock. By forecasting sales and providing your suppliers with accurate information, you can collaborate to ensure timely restocking and avoid costly delays.

Additionally, consider diversifying your supplier base. Relying on a single supplier can put your business at risk if they experience production issues or delays. Having multiple suppliers provides a safety net, reducing the chances of stockouts during unforeseen circumstances.

4. Set Reorder Points:
A reorder point is the predetermined inventory level at which you should place an order with your supplier to replenish stock. It acts as a signal that triggers

reordering, ensuring you maintain optimal inventory levels and avoid stockouts. Establishing reorder points based on historical sales data and lead times can help streamline your inventory management process.

When setting reorder points, consider factors such as shipping times, supplier lead times, and expected sales velocity. By properly calibrating these points, you can minimize the risk of stockouts while avoiding excessive inventory holding costs.

5. Utilize Backorder Options:
In cases where a particular product is out of stock, offering backorders can be a viable solution. When customers place a backorder, they understand that the product will be shipped to them once it becomes available again. This allows you to capture sales even when inventory is temporarily depleted.

Ensure clear communication with customers when offering backorders. Set realistic expectations for when the product will be restocked and provide regular updates on the progress. With proper management, backorders can be an effective strategy to maintain customer satisfaction and maximize revenue potential.

6. Consider Safety Stock:
Safety stock acts as a buffer to guard against unexpected fluctuations in demand or delays in restocking. It represents additional inventory held above the reorder point and provides a cushion to bridge the gap between supply and demand.

Estimating safety stock requires analyzing demand volatility, supplier performance, and lead times. While safety stock increases holding costs, it provides a safety net and helps prevent stockouts during unforeseen circumstances.

Managing inventory and avoiding stockouts is an ongoing process that requires attention, analysis, and adaptation. By implementing these strategies and constantly monitoring your inventory performance, you can mitigate the challenges associated with inventory management and ensure your dropshipping business operates smoothly.

Remember, efficient inventory management not only helps you maintain customer satisfaction, but it also maximizes your revenue potential by capturing sales opportunities and minimizing costs associated with stockouts and excessive inventory.

Handling Customer Complaints and Disputes

In any business, there will inevitably be situations where customers have complaints or disputes. As a dropshipping entrepreneur, it's crucial to have a solid strategy for handling these issues to maintain customer satisfaction and protect your brand's reputation. In this section, we will delve into effective methods for resolving customer complaints and disputes in a professional and efficient manner.

1. Promptly Respond to Customer Inquiries:
When a customer reaches out with a complaint or dispute, it is essential to acknowledge their concerns promptly. Ignoring or delaying a response can escalate the situation and lead to negative reviews or feedback. Aim to address the customer within 24 hours, expressing empathy and a commitment to resolving the issue.

2. Listen and Understand:
When communicating with a dissatisfied customer, it's crucial to listen actively and understand their perspective. Allow them to express their concerns fully and avoid interrupting or becoming defensive. Show empathy, demonstrating that you genuinely care about their experience and are committed to finding a resolution.

3. Offer a Solution:
After understanding the customer's complaint or dispute, work towards offering a solution that addresses their needs. Offer a range of possible solutions and let the customer choose the option that best suits them. This approach helps empower the customer and increases the likelihood of a satisfactory outcome.

4. Provide Regular Updates:
Once a solution is underway, communicate regularly with the customer to keep them informed about the progress. This demonstrates your commitment to resolving the issue and ensures that the customer feels involved in the process. Even if there are delays or

setbacks, honesty and transparency are critical to maintaining trust.

5. Go Above and Beyond:
To turn a potentially negative experience into a positive one, consider going the extra mile for your customers. This can include offering a small discount, a freebie, or an apology gift. These gestures show that you value their business and are willing to make amends for any inconvenience caused.

6. Document Everything:
Keep detailed records of all customer complaints and the steps taken to resolve them. This documentation can serve as evidence in case any disputes escalate further. It is also helpful for monitoring patterns and identifying areas for improvement in your business processes.

7. Learn from Mistakes:
When handling customer complaints and disputes, view them as opportunities for growth and improvement. Analyze the root causes of the complaints and take steps to prevent similar issues from arising in the future. Continuously refining your processes will also help reduce the frequency of complaints, thus improving overall customer satisfaction.

8. Utilize Customer Feedback:
Encourage customers to provide feedback about their experience with your store, products, and customer service. This can be done through email surveys, pop-up forms, or by creating a dedicated feedback section on

your website. Actively listen to customer feedback and use it to enhance your business practices. Positive feedback can be testimonials to showcase, while negative feedback can guide you in making necessary improvements.

Handling customer complaints and disputes is an inevitable part of running a dropshipping business. By promptly responding to inquiries, listening and understanding customer perspectives, offering solutions, providing regular updates, going above and beyond, documenting everything, learning from mistakes, and utilizing customer feedback, you can effectively resolve issues and maintain customer satisfaction. Remember, every complaint presents an opportunity to improve your business and demonstrate your commitment to exceptional customer service.

Chapter 10: Financial Management and Profit Maximization

In this chapter, we will dive into the crucial topic of financial management and profit maximization. As an aspiring dropshipper, it's essential to have a solid understanding of pricing strategies for competitive advantage. By optimizing costs, tracking expenses and revenue, and implementing strategies to increase profitability, you can set your Shopify store up for success. So, let's get started!

Pricing Strategies for Competitive Advantage

When it comes to dropshipping, pricing your products strategically can give you a competitive edge in the market. Here are some tried-and-tested pricing strategies to help you maximize profit while attracting customers:

1. Cost-Plus Pricing:
Cost-plus pricing involves adding a fixed percentage or dollar amount to your product's cost to determine its selling price. This method ensures that you cover your costs while generating a profit. To implement cost-plus pricing effectively, you need to calculate all your expenses, including product costs, shipping fees, transaction fees, marketing expenses, and any other

overhead costs. By factoring in all these costs and applying a suitable margin, you can determine a profitable selling price.

Example:
Let's say you sourced a product for $10, your shipping costs are $2, and you have $3 in additional expenses (transaction fees, marketing, etc.). With a desired profit margin of 40%, you would add $6 ($10 x 40%) to your costs, resulting in a selling price of $21 ($10 + $2 + $3 + $6).

2. Psychological Pricing:
Psychological pricing exploits human psychology to influence purchasing decisions. By setting prices slightly lower or slightly higher than round numbers, you can create the illusion of a better deal or higher quality. Here are two commonly used psychological pricing strategies:

    a. Charm Pricing: Set prices at just below a whole number (e.g., $9.99 instead of $10). This pricing strategy capitalizes on the psychological perception that $9.99 seems significantly lower than $10, even though it's only a one cent difference.

    b. Prestige Pricing: Set prices slightly higher to convey exclusivity, premium quality, or luxury. Customers often perceive higher-priced products as having superior value. Be mindful of your target market and ensure that your products and branding align with a higher price point.

Example:
Consider selling a trendy phone case. Instead of pricing it at $10, you can employ charm pricing and set it at $9.99. This price conveys a significant difference in perception, making it appear cheaper to potential buyers.

3. Bundle Pricing:
Bundle pricing involves offering complementary products as a bundle at a discounted price compared to purchasing each item separately. This strategy encourages customers to buy more items, increasing the average order value and your profit margin. By bundling related products that complement each other, you can provide added value to customers while boosting your sales.

Example:
If you sell skincare products, you might bundle a cleanser, toner, and moisturizer together at a discounted price compared to buying them individually. This bundle pricing strategy entices customers to purchase the entire set rather than just one product, increasing your revenue.

4. Dynamic Pricing:
Dynamic pricing involves adjusting prices based on market demand, competition, or even the time of day. This strategy allows you to maximize profits by charging higher prices during peak demand periods and lower prices during off-peak times. Monitoring market trends and using pricing analysis tools can help you determine when to adjust your prices for maximum profit.

Example:
If you notice that a certain product is in high demand during the holiday season, you can increase its price to align with customer willingness to pay during that period. Conversely, during slower sales periods, you might consider lowering prices to attract more customers.

Remember, pricing strategies require ongoing evaluation and adjustment. Regularly analyze your sales data, monitor market trends, and test different pricing approaches to find the optimal balance between profitability and attracting customers.

(Note: The examples provided are for illustrative purposes only. It's essential to conduct thorough market research, understand your costs, and gather real-time data to make informed pricing decisions.)

Cost Optimization and Margin Improvement

In this section, let's explore the crucial aspects of cost optimization and margin improvement to help you maximize your profit potential in the dropshipping business.

Cost Optimization:
When running a dropshipping business, it's essential to minimize costs without compromising the quality of your products or the satisfaction of your customers. Here are some strategies you can employ to optimize costs:

1. Supplier Negotiations: Build strong relationships with your suppliers and negotiate better rates for your products. As your business grows, you'll have more purchasing power, allowing you to secure favorable terms and pricing.

2. Bulk Ordering: Consider ordering products in larger quantities to take advantage of volume discounts. By doing so, you can reduce your per-unit costs and increase your profit margins.

3. Inventory Management: Implement an efficient inventory management system to avoid overstocking or running out of popular items. Reducing storage costs and minimizing losses due to unsold inventory can significantly impact your profitability.

4. Shipping Optimization: Evaluate shipping options and negotiate lower rates with shipping carriers. Integrating with fulfillment services can help streamline the shipping process, reducing costs and improving customer satisfaction.

Margin Improvement:
Increasing your profit margins is vital for long-term success in the dropshipping business. Here are some strategies to consider:

1. Product Selection: Carefully curate your product offerings to focus on high-margin items. Identify products with low competition and high demand that can be sold at a premium price.

2. Upselling and Cross-selling: Encourage customers to purchase additional items or upgrade their orders by showcasing complementary products. Bundling products together or offering exclusive deals can increase the average order value, boosting margins.

3. Value-Added Services: Explore opportunities to provide value-added services, such as customization, gift wrapping, or faster shipping options. These additional services can be offered at a higher price point, increasing your margins.

4. Branding and Differentiation: Build a strong brand identity and focus on differentiating yourself from the competition. Develop a unique selling proposition that resonates with your target audience, allowing you to command higher prices.

Tracking Expenses and Revenue

Accurate tracking of your expenses and revenue is crucial for understanding the financial health of your dropshipping business. Here's how you can effectively track and analyze your finances:

1. Accounting Software: Utilize accounting software, such as QuickBooks or Xero, to streamline your financial management. These tools can help you track your expenses, revenue, and profit margins more efficiently.

2. Cost Breakdown: Categorize and track your expenses, including product costs, advertising expenses, transaction fees, shipping costs, software subscriptions, and other operational expenses. Having a clear breakdown of your costs will help identify areas that need optimization.

3. Revenue Analysis: Monitor your revenue streams, including sales from your Shopify store, affiliate programs, or any other channels. Identify your best-performing products and focus on scaling those to maximize your profitability.

4. Financial Reports: Regularly generate financial reports, such as profit and loss statements and cash flow statements, to gain a comprehensive overview of your business's financial performance. Make sure to analyze these reports to identify trends, spot areas for improvement, this is important to help you make data-driven decisions.

Remember, cost optimization and margin improvement require continuous evaluation and adjustment. Regularly assess your expenses, revenue, and profit margins to identify opportunities for improvement and stay ahead of the competition.

By implementing these strategies and closely monitoring your financials, you'll be well on your way to maximizing your profit potential in the dropshipping business.

Strategies for Increasing Profitability

Congratulations! By implementing the dropshipping business model and managing your finances effectively, you are well on your way to building a successful Shopify store. In this section, we will explore strategies that can help you increase your profitability and maximize your earnings. These proven methods will help you take your dropshipping business to the next level.

1. Expand Your Product Range:

Once you have established a solid foundation with your initial product line, consider expanding it to attract a wider customer base. Conduct market research to identify popular products within your niche that align with your brand and target audience. By diversifying your offering, you can attract new customers and increase your overall revenue.

2. Upsell and Cross-sell:

Take advantage of the opportunity to increase your average order value by implementing upselling and cross-selling techniques. Upselling involves offering customers a higher-priced item or an upgraded version of the product they are considering. Cross-selling, on the other hand, involves suggesting complementary products that enhance the customer's original purchase. By utilizing these techniques, you can maximize your revenue per customer transaction.

3. Implement Effective Marketing Strategies:

Investing in targeted marketing is crucial to drive traffic to your Shopify store and increase conversion rates. Experiment with various marketing channels, such as social media advertising, influencer partnerships, search engine optimization, and email marketing. Analyze the performance of each channel and focus on the ones that yield the highest returns for your business.

4. Build Customer Loyalty:

It is more cost-effective to retain current customers than to acquire new ones. Foster customer loyalty by providing exceptional customer service, offering incentives for repeat purchases, and implementing a customer loyalty program. These efforts will not only increase customer satisfaction but also generate repeat business, leading to improved profitability in the long run.

5. Optimize Your Pricing Strategy:

Carefully analyze your pricing strategy to find the sweet spot that maximizes your profits. Consider factors such as product costs, competitor pricing, and perceived customer value. Experiment with different pricing models, such as cost-plus pricing, value-based pricing, or even dynamic pricing. Monitor the performance of your pricing strategy and make adjustments accordingly.

6. Reduce Costs:

Identify areas where you can reduce costs without compromising on the quality of your products or customer experience. Negotiate better deals with suppliers, optimize your inventory management to minimize waste, and explore cost-effective shipping options. By reducing your expenses, you can increase your profit margins and improve your overall profitability.

7. Optimize Conversion Rates:

Improving your website's conversion rates can significantly impact your bottom line. Implement effective user experience design, ensure your website is mobile-friendly, and streamline the checkout process to reduce cart abandonment. Split testing different versions of your website or individual product pages can help you identify and implement changes that lead to higher conversion rates.

8. Utilize Data Analytics:

Make data-driven decisions by regularly analyzing key performance indicators (KPIs) such as average order value, customer acquisition cost, and conversion rates. Leverage the power of data analytics tools, such as

Google Analytics or Shopify's built-in analytics, to gain valuable insights into your business's performance. These insights can help you identify areas for improvement and implement strategies to increase profitability.

Remember, increasing profitability is a journey, and it requires continuous evaluation, experimentation, and adaptation. Implementing these strategies will provide you with a solid foundation for maximizing your earnings. By combining them with your dedication and hard work, your dropshipping business has the potential to flourish and become a profitable venture.

Stay focused, keep learning, and never hesitate to try new techniques and ideas. Every step you take towards increasing your profitability will bring you closer to achieving your financial goals. Good luck, and may your Shopify store thrive and prosper!

Chapter 11: Future Trends and Strategies

Adapting to Evolving E-Commerce Trends

Keeping up with the latest trends is essential for achieving success in this fast-paced competitive e-commerce industry.

As technology advances and consumer behaviors change, it's essential to adapt to the evolving trends in the industry. In this section, we will explore some key trends and strategies that can help you stay ahead and continue to generate revenue through your dropshipping Shopify store.

1. Mobile Commerce (M-Commerce)
With the growing popularity of smartphones and tablets, mobile commerce, or m-commerce, has become an integral part of the e-commerce landscape. As more people rely on their mobile devices for online shopping, it's important to optimize your Shopify store for mobile users. Ensure that your website is mobile responsive, user-friendly, and offers a seamless buying experience across different screen sizes. By prioritizing mobile optimization, you can cater to a wider audience and increase your sales potential.

2. Voice Search Optimization

Voice assistants like Siri, Alexa, and Google Assistant have revolutionized how people search for information online. Voice search is becoming increasingly popular, and it's estimated that by 2024, around half of all internet searches will be done through voice commands. To adapt to this trend, optimize your Shopify store for voice search by incorporating long-tail keywords and answering common search queries within your product descriptions and blog posts. By doing so, you increase your chances of appearing in voice search results and capturing voice-driven sales leads.

3. Personalization and AI-driven Recommendations
Today, customers have higher expectations and desire personalized shopping experiences based on their individual preferences. AI-driven technologies can help you analyze customer data to understand their behavior, preferences, and shopping patterns. Use this information to create personalized product recommendations and offer targeted promotions. Shopify provides several apps and plugins that integrate seamlessly with your store, offering AI-driven recommendation engines. By leveraging personalization and AI, you can increase customer engagement, loyalty, and ultimately boost your revenue.

4. Social Commerce and Influencer Marketing
Social media platforms have become primary channels for businesses to engage with their target audience. Integrating your Shopify store with popular social media platforms like Instagram and Facebook can help you reach a wider audience and drive more traffic to your

store. In addition, influencer marketing has gained significant traction in recent years. Collaborating with social media influencers who have a relevant audience can greatly benefit your dropshipping business. They can promote your products, generate brand awareness, and drive conversions. It's important to select influencers for collaborations who share the same values as your brand and have followers that align with your target audience.

5. Sustainable and Ethical Practices
More consumers than ever before are actively seeking brands that prioritize sustainability and ethical practices. Incorporate environmentally friendly initiatives into your business model, such as eco-friendly packaging, carbon-offset shipping, or partnering with charitable organizations. Communicate these practices to your customers through your website and marketing campaigns. By demonstrating your commitment to sustainability, you can appeal to conscious consumers and build a loyal customer base.

Remember, it's essential to stay updated on the latest e-commerce trends to keep your dropshipping business thriving. Continuously monitor industry news, attend webinars, and participate in relevant forums or communities to stay informed. By adapting to evolving e-commerce trends and implementing innovative strategies, you can position your dropshipping Shopify store for sustained success in the ever-changing online marketplace.

Next, let's explore new opportunities and platforms that can help expand your reach and generate more revenue for your dropshipping business.

Exploring New Opportunities and Platforms

In addition to adapting to evolving e-commerce trends, exploring new opportunities and platforms can help you expand your reach and generate more revenue for your dropshipping business. Let's dive into some of these opportunities and strategies to maximize your success.

1. Expansion into Emerging Markets
As the internet becomes more accessible worldwide, there is a growing opportunity to tap into emerging markets. Countries like India, Brazil, and Indonesia are experiencing significant growth in e-commerce. Consider expanding your dropshipping business to these markets by localizing your website, accepting local payment options, and tailoring your product offerings to meet local demands. Conduct market research to understand the unique characteristics and preferences of these regions to maximize your chances of success.

2. Multi-Channel Selling
While Shopify is an excellent platform for your dropshipping business, expanding your presence to multiple sales channels can increase your customer reach and sales potential. Explore other popular e-commerce platforms like Amazon, eBay, or Walmart Marketplace to sell your products. By diversifying your sales

channels, you can capture a broader audience and leverage the customer base and infrastructure of these established platforms. Use tools like Shopify's integrations or third-party apps to seamlessly manage inventory, orders, and listings across multiple channels.

3. Automated Email Marketing
Email marketing is a powerful tool for nurturing customer relationships and driving repeat sales. Implementing automated email marketing campaigns can help you engage with your customers at various stages of the buyer's journey. Set up email sequences triggered by specific actions, such as abandoned cart reminders, post-purchase follow-ups, or personalized product recommendations. By delivering targeted and relevant content to your customers' inbox, you can increase customer retention, repeat purchases, and overall revenue.

4. Virtual Reality (VR) and Augmented Reality (AR)
Augmented Reality (AR) and Virtual Reality (VR) have revolutionized the way people shop online, enhancing their overall experience. By integrating AR and VR features into your Shopify store, you can provide customers with a virtual try-on experience for clothing or allow them to visualize how your products might look in their space. AR and VR can enhance customer engagement, reduce purchase hesitation, and improve overall customer satisfaction. Several Shopify apps and plugins make it easy to implement AR/VR features into your store without requiring extensive technical knowledge or large investments.

5. Subscription-Based Model
The subscription-based business model has gained immense popularity in recent years. Consider offering subscription boxes or membership programs to your customers. This model allows you to create a recurring revenue stream and increase customer loyalty. Depending on your niche, you can curate a unique collection of products, provide exclusive benefits, or offer personalized experiences to your subscription customers. Implementing a subscription-based model can help you build predictable revenue and deepen customer relationships.

6. Blockchain Technology for Transparency
Blockchain technology has the potential to revolutionize e-commerce by providing transparency and trust in supply chains. Consider leveraging blockchain to ensure the authenticity of your products, trace their origins, and provide verifiable information about their ethical and sustainable practices. Incorporating blockchain technology can resonate with conscious consumers who value transparency and accountability. Several blockchain-based platforms exist, such as Provenance or VeChain, that can help you implement these features into your dropshipping business.

By exploring new opportunities and platforms, you can unlock untapped potential for your dropshipping business and stay at the forefront of the evolving e-commerce landscape. Evaluate these strategies that resonate with your business model and industry, and implement them strategically to achieve sustainable growth and profitability.

Chapter 12: Conclusion

Congratulations on reaching the final chapter of "Dropshipping Shopify 2024!".

Throughout this detailed and informative guide, you have acquired valuable insights and knowledge on how to create a successful Shopify store, starting from the beginning, and earning consistent monthly revenue through the profitable dropshipping e-commerce business model. Now, let's recap the key learnings and provide you with tips for success in dropshipping on Shopify in 2024.

Recap of Key Learnings

1. Understanding Dropshipping:

By utilizing the dropshipping business model, you can sell products online without the need for inventory or upfront costs. You act as a middleman, connecting customers with suppliers, and earning a profit from the margin between your wholesale purchase price and the retail price you set.

2. Selecting a Profitable Niche:

Finding a profitable niche is is very important for your success in dropshipping. Research market trends, identify customer pain points, and choose a niche that aligns with your passion and target audience. Validate your niche by conducting market research and competitor analysis.

3. Building a Professional Shopify Store:

Shopify is an excellent highly effective platform that provides exceptional capabilities for creating, building and managing your online store. Begin by selecting an appealing theme and customizing it to reflect your brand. Optimize your store for mobile devices, ensure easy navigation, and write compelling product descriptions. Be sure to use high-quality & compelling images and videos to showcase your products effectively.

4. Sourcing Reliable Suppliers:

Establishing strong relationships with trustworthy suppliers is very important. Work with suppliers who offer competitive pricing, quality products, and efficient shipping methods. Review supplier ratings and engage in open communication to ensure smooth operations.

5. Implementing Effective Marketing Strategies:

To drive traffic and generate sales, leverage various marketing strategies such as social media advertising, influencer partnerships, email marketing, and search engine optimization (SEO). Be sure to utilize analytics tools to measure the effectiveness of your marketing campaigns, this help you to make data-driven decisions which is compulsory.

6. Providing Excellent Customer Service:

Providing exceptional customer service is essential to building & maintaining a loyal customer base. Respond promptly to customer inquiries, provide accurate product information, and handle returns and refunds professionally. Personalize the customer experience and nurture relationships for long-term success.

7. Scaling Your Business:
As you gain momentum, it's essential to scale your business. Optimize your product offerings, expand into new markets, and consider implementing automation tools to streamline your processes. Continuously test and optimize your strategies to maximize profitability.

Tips for Success in Dropshipping on Shopify in 2024

1. Stay on Top of Industry Trends:
The e-commerce industry is constantly evolving, and staying informed about the latest trends is crucial for your success. Keep an eye on emerging technologies, new marketing platforms, and changes in consumer behavior. Stay connected with industry publications, follow influencers, and join relevant communities to stay ahead of the curve.

2. Embrace Automation Tools:
As your business grows, manual tasks can become overwhelming. Embrace automation tools to streamline your operations and save time. Tools like inventory management software, chatbots, and email marketing

automation can help you automate repetitive tasks, improve efficiency, and provide a better customer experience.

3. Build a Strong Brand:
Building a strong brand can undoubtedly separate you from the competition, especially in this highly competitive e-commerce industry. Develop a distinctive brand identity that strongly connects with your intended audience. Create a compelling brand story, design a memorable logo, and establish consistent visual and verbal brand elements across all your marketing channels.

4. Offer Exceptional Customer Support:
Customer support plays a crucial role in the success of an e-commerce business. Provide exceptional customer support by offering multiple channels for communication, such as live chat, email, and social media. Respond promptly and professionally to customer inquiries, resolve issues quickly, and strive to exceed customer expectations.

5. Optimize for Mobile:
More and more consumers are shopping on their mobile devices, so it's essential to optimize your Shopify store for mobile. Make sure that your website is responsive and loads quickly on mobile devices. Test the user experience across different screen sizes and regularly optimize to provide a seamless mobile shopping experience.

6. Leverage Social Media Advertising:
Social media platforms like Facebook and Instagram offer powerful advertising options to reach your target audience. Develop a social media advertising strategy that aligns with your business goals and create visually appealing ad creatives. Use targeting options to reach your ideal customers and track your ad performance to optimize your campaigns.

7. Implement Influencer Marketing:
A well-executed influencer marketing campaign can help expand your reach to a larger audience and establish trust with potential customers. Identify influencers in your niche who have an engaged audience, and collaborate with them to promote your products. Create unique partnerships and track the performance of each influencer to ensure a positive return on investment.

8. Leverage User-Generated Content:
User-generated content (UGC) is an excellent way to build trust and authenticity. Encourage your customers to share their experiences with your products by incentivizing them with discounts or contests. Share UGC on your website and social media platforms, showcasing real-life testimonials to attract new customers.

9. Continuously Test and Optimize:
Successful dropshipping businesses are always looking for ways to improve. Use analytics tools like Google Analytics and Shopify's built-in analytics to track your store's performance. Conduct A/B tests on your website,

ads, and landing pages to discover what works best for your target audience and optimize accordingly.

10. Stay Committed and Persistent:
Building a successful dropshipping business takes time, effort, and persistence. Stay committed to your goals, maintain a positive mindset, and don't get discouraged by setbacks. Remember to learn from your mistakes, be adaptable in your strategies, and stay persistent. Consistency and perseverance are absolutely crucial in order to attain long-term success.

With these tips in mind, you're well-equipped to navigate the world of dropshipping on Shopify in 2024. Remember, success in e-commerce doesn't happen overnight, but with dedication, hard work, and a customer-centric approach, you can build a profitable business and achieve your goals. Happy dropshipping!

In conclusion, this guide has offered you a clear path to excel in the dropshipping e-commerce sector, specifically by utilizing Shopify effectively.

By understanding the key learnings, implementing effective strategies, and embracing tips for success, you're well-equipped to navigate the dynamic world of dropshipping on Shopify in 2024 and beyond. So launch your Shopify store, step into the world of e-commerce, and transform your dreams into a profitable reality!

Don't forget to start implementing what you learnt in this guide immediately.

I hope the tips provided in this guide have been helpful to you in your journey as a dropshipper on Shopify. If you found this information valuable, I would greatly appreciate it if you could take a moment to leave a review on Amazon. Your review will not only help others who are looking for guidance in dropshipping but also enable me to better cater to your needs in the future.

Printed in Great Britain
by Amazon

48706827R00059